MAKING PICTURE-BOOKS

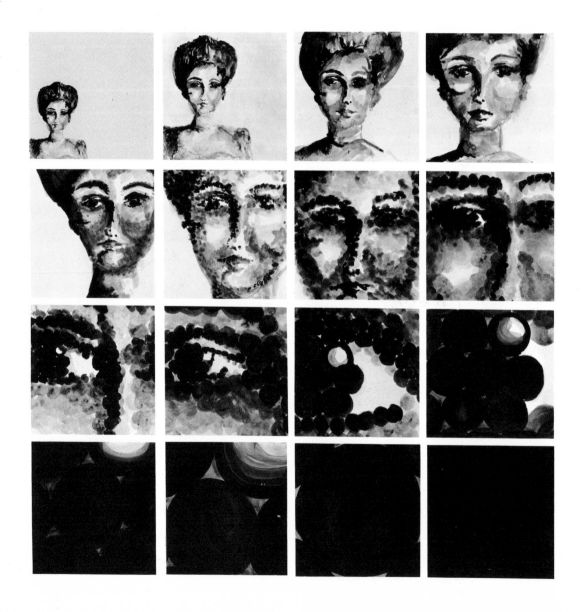

MAKING PICTURE-BOOKS

A Method of Learning Graphic Sequence

Stephen F. Gordon

An Art Horizons Book

Van Nostrand Reinhold Company
New York Cincinnati Toronto London Melbourne

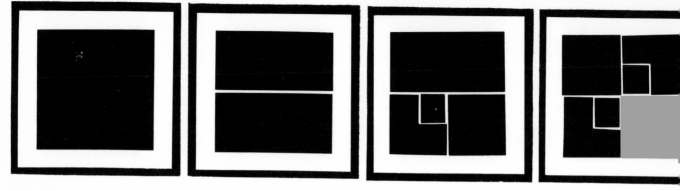

To Dori & Jenine

All of the artwork in this book was done by
students in the author's classes at White Plains
High School, White Plains, New York.

Van Nostrand Reinhold Company Regional Offices:
New York, Cincinnati, Chicago, Millbrae, Dallas
Van Nostrand Reinhold Company Foreign Offices:
London, Toronto, Melbourne

Design consultant: Milton Glaser
Type set by V & M Typographical, Inc.
Printed by Halliday Lithograph Corporation
Bound by Publishers Book Bindery, Inc.

Published by Van Nostrand Reinhold Company,
450 West 33rd Street, New York, N.Y. 10001
Published simultaneously in Canada by
D. Van Nostrand Company (Canada), Ltd.

16 15 14 13 12 11 10 9 8 7 6 5 4 3 2 1

Also by the author, with Jenifer D. Wyman:
A Primer of Perception (1967)

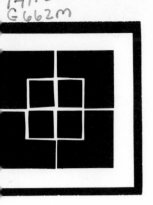

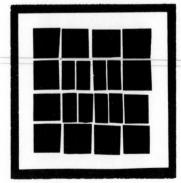

Contents

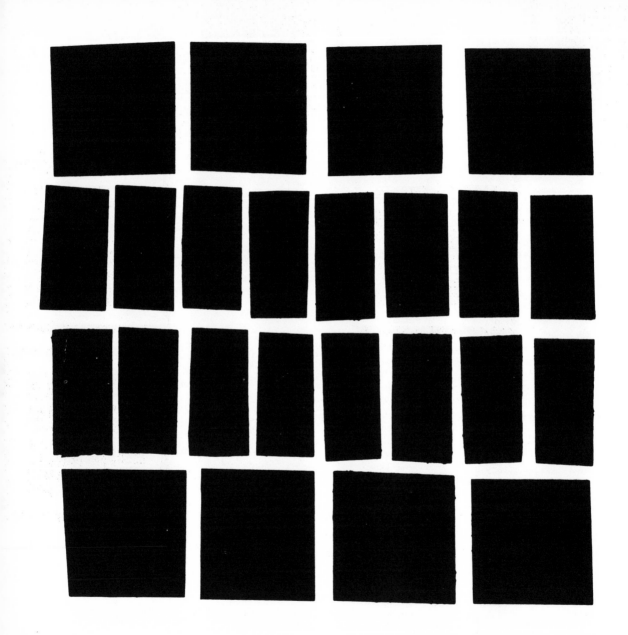

Introduction

A picture-book is composed of images that have been placed in a sequence which has special visual meaning. The student who makes one of these books will learn the qualities of sequence, how sequence builds up new design forces, and how the experience of sequence in art differs from the tradition of experiencing a single work of art.

Contemporary man is a "visual" man. Visual images surround us and move through us like rays, simultaneously making a record of themselves and recording what we are. Images are inseparable from our souls; the two together are like those windows composed of layers of plastic and glass wedded by machinery into a complementary and indeterminate bond. It is through this window composed of image and self that all our experiences appear. We thus are what we see, and how we see is crucial to what we see.

The "how" of vision is an enormous subject. But in one particular area it is changing more rapidly than in others: the extent of our experience in the area of sequential vision is increasing enormously. No vision is static, of course.

Everyone realizes this and moves his eyes to see the parts of an image or walks around an object to see all its sides. But we are increasingly immersed in vision which responds to a sequence of images.

What are the sources of sequential imagery, and what do they have in common? Obviously film and TV have had a pervasive effect on the visual experience of man, but we must also consider the fragmentary way we see as we move rapidly in contemporary machines. Consider too the exhibit systems that build up their effects as the viewer moves through them; projection systems, especially those that use more than one screen and image at a time; sound and light shows; and, of course, the new image books—books with overlays that show how parts of things fit together, books of the new photo-journalism, books that are more viewed than read.

All of these sources of imagery have in common the quality of building up their impact by showing only part of the total at any one time. Furthermore, each image builds from, and relates to, each of the other images that have

been shown. The total cumulative image exists only in the mind of the viewer. Naturally each individual image, at the time it is seen, is similar to all other static images in that the eye of the viewer moves over it and evaluates it. But in the case of the new imagery, the additional fundamental quality for the viewer to experience is the change or growth of the image. Yet most art is still either formed or taught in terms of a single, static image.

This anachronism may be eliminated through the use of the sequential image book as art and as a teaching form. Such a book can be unfolded and experienced in a variety of ways, and its construction is a relatively inexpensive project for the artist or student. A book has the potential for sequential growth not only because it unfolds, but also because it has the added quality of unfolding at the rate of selection of the viewer and can be constructed to do so in any combination of directions or shapes that the designer of the book can devise.

We now face a basic question:

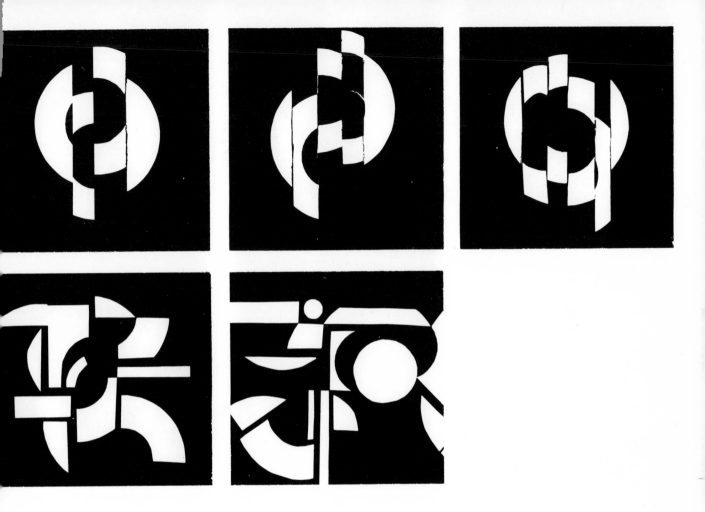

HOW DOES ONE MAKE A PICTURE-BOOK?

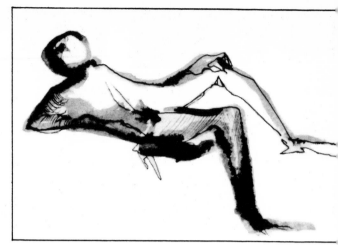

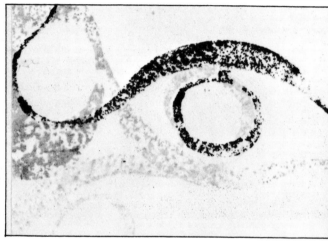

1.

How to Make a Picture-Book: Subject, Style, and Theme

The best beginning is to dismiss any preconceptions as to what is the historically proper or logical form of a book. The clay tablets from Crete are ancient books. The Egyptians carved and painted their book-images on monumental pyramids as well as on the narrow passageways within them. A spectator was required to walk up stairs around Trajan's Column in Rome in order to follow the sequence of its images. In contemporary times, books have been composed on paper, parchment, plastic, and metal; by hand printing and by enormous presses; they have been glued, tied, hole-punched, or heat-pressed together, or boxed unbound—in short, books are produced by a multitude of techniques and approaches.

Content is equally varied. The charm of a book is that it can be about anything. It can cover the girth of elephants or the enormousness of space on the few inches of a page. There are no prohibitions on subject or style or theme. It need only have a start. Take a flower. You already have a subject that has a life cycle of growth, a form of its own for style, and any number of other themes in its color, roots, texture, etc.

The first step in making a book is to determine with gloriously pure clarity what it is going to be about. Then attempt to divide that deftly into subject, style, or theme. This chapter depicts how those sections—subject, style, or theme—can be handled.

The subject, whatever idea or topic or image it may be, should be made up of repeated forms. It should lead the viewer forward with these shapes and should have some sort of drama building in scale or detail. As a sample of a subject, we have used the human figure and have indicated how a random group of sketches might be organized to become a story sequence.

Style is very hard to define but clear to see. It is a form of consistency, an effort on the part of the designer to keep the elements of his book in sympathetic association. This may be a relationship of color or texture, or it may be an interweaving of similar technique or design approach. Does the subject imply something contemporary or romantic, baroque or classic? And in what materials—ink, collage, wood print, watercolor? Whatever its impetus, style becomes the life force that binds the images together.

The theme of a book is even more difficult to define and less clearly discernible. It is not just the subject or the style, and yet it is related to both. In some cases it is basically a subject that is very subtle and thus does not appear to be the sharply defined center of attention. Or the theme might explore a mood or analyze how an object or idea unfolds, for example, the study of a color or an emotion.

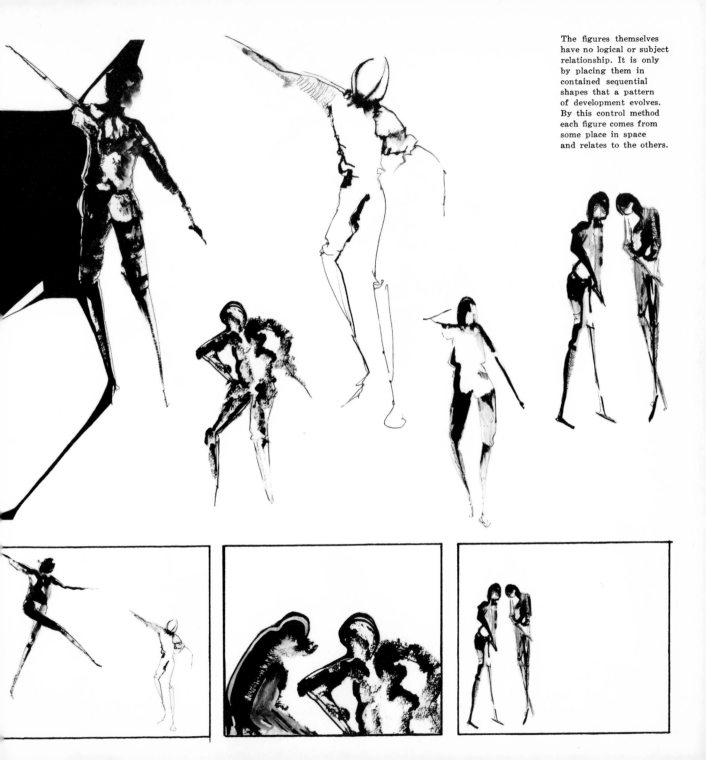

The figures themselves
have no logical or subject
relationship. It is only
by placing them in
contained sequential
shapes that a pattern
of development evolves.
By this control method
each figure comes from
some place in space
and relates to the others.

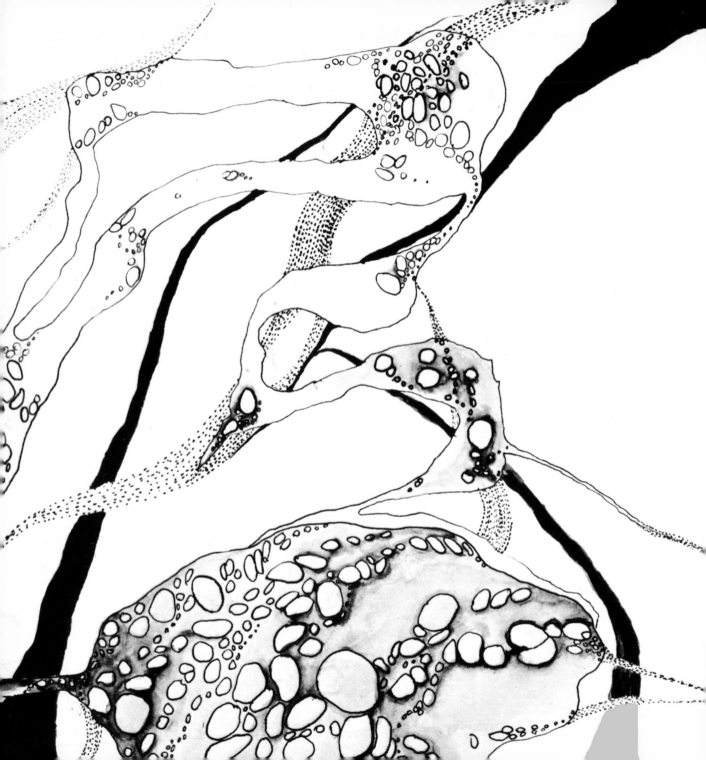

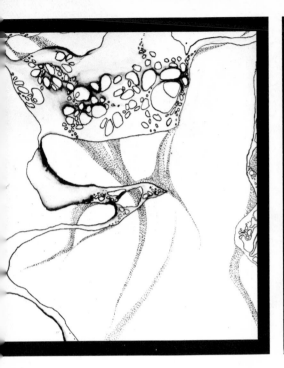

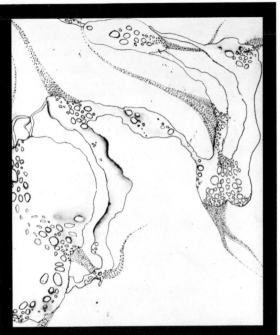

The style of these samples of sequential art is clear. The variations on a set visual idea allow the style to be even more manifest than it would be in a single-image presentation. The style is composed of both materials (ink and wash in one case, cut-out cork shapes and watercolor in the other) and drawing technique.

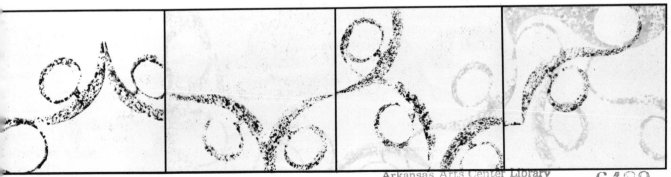

In contrast to the subtlety of the preceding styles, this group of drawings shows a hard, sharp style. However, once the style has been established, it follows an indefinable but clear logic in all of the variations done within that style.

A theme is difficult to distinguish from a style or a subject. Perhaps they are all so intertwined that clear contrasts are impossible with visual images. To the extent that it helps comprehension, this is a theme because it grows around an idea (in this case a line that bleeds shapes from itself).

18

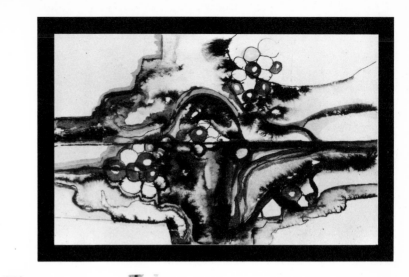

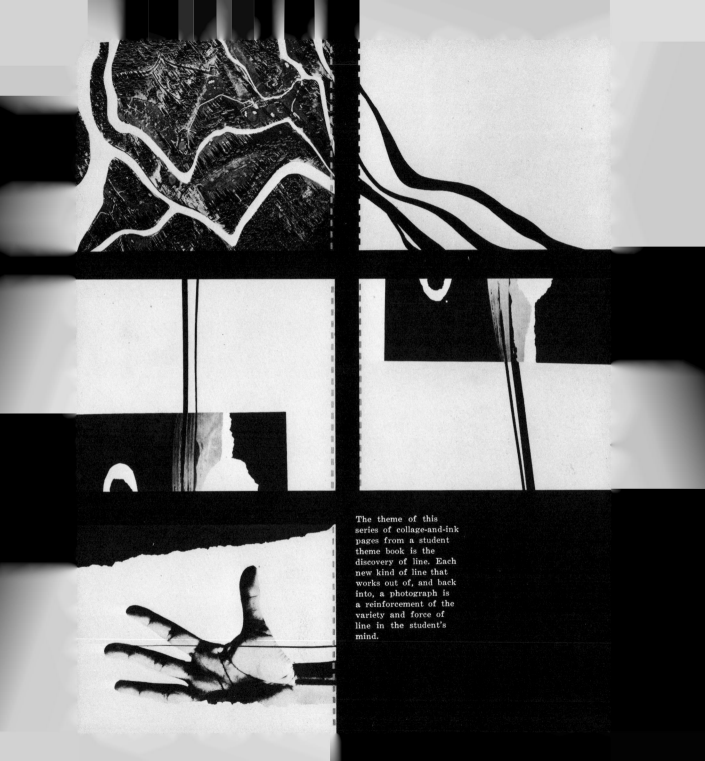

The theme of this series of collage-and-ink pages from a student theme book is the discovery of line. Each new kind of line that works out of, and back into, a photograph is a reinforcement of the variety and force of line in the student's mind.

The sequence of hands
moving illustrates all
the considerations of this
chapter simultaneously:
namely, the subject
(black and white hand),
the style (ink line),
and the theme (moving
together and meshing).
The other series is a
slightly more complicated
example of the three
elements working
together.

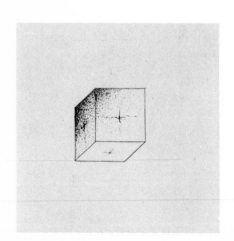  

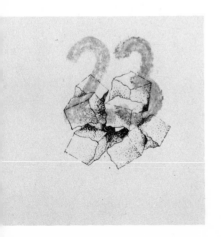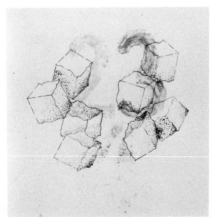

2.
Shapes

he shape of a book has no magic
otency to fulfill the intention of the
rtist. At best it can offer only a subtle
attery to the subject, style, or theme.
either is there any pattern of logic
s to which shapes support which ideas.
ut there is a clear mandate to use a
ariety of shapes, to experiment with
hapes, and to attempt to blend form
nd content in a book as much as in,
or example, architecture.

All of the shapes and diagrams of
this chapter are designed to suggest
some of the range or potential of book
shapes. They illustrate the idea that a
book can open in many directions, that
it can be composed of differently
formed parts, and that it can range
from the subtle to the dramatic in size,
pattern, or manner of unfolding.
A book that shows only one page at

a time is modest compared to one that
grows in size as it opens. A book that
has many alternative arrangements
is far more sophisticated than one that
can open in only one direction.

The basic shapes given on this page
indicate only some of the starting points
from which books can vary and grow.
The example on the facing page is
one of the many alternatives to
geometric shapes.

These pages are squares
of equal size which
have been bound together
with tape. The advantage
of using tape rather
than simply folding
is that it permits the
student to move the units
until he decides on the
sequence that he wants.

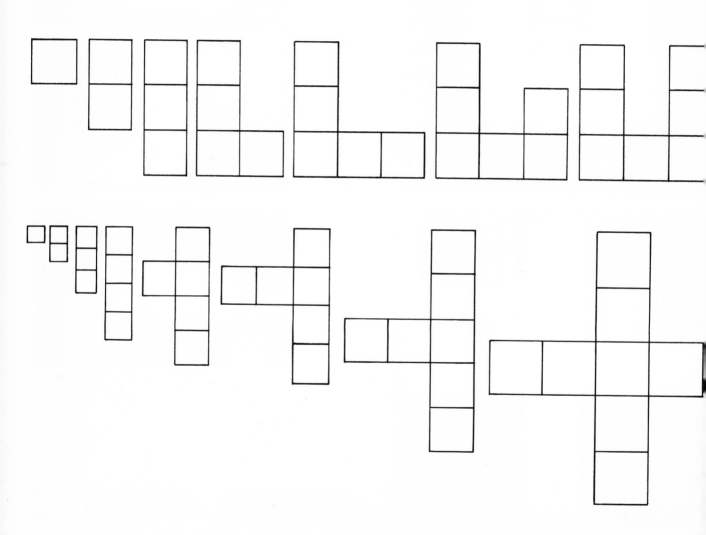

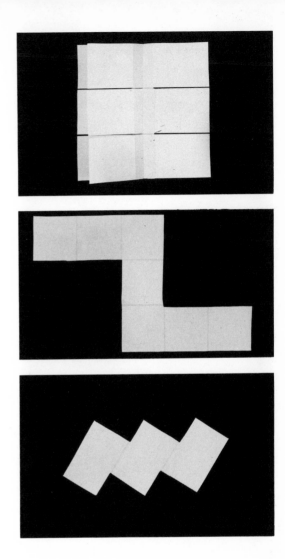

As the elemental square shape is opened in the samples on this page, it becomes a much more interesting and involved form. It makes possible the use of the book as an image growing in size and direction. As each new page is turned open it changes the total effect. Even when the book is finally open, it is not a static object, for it is then waiting to be closed image by image.

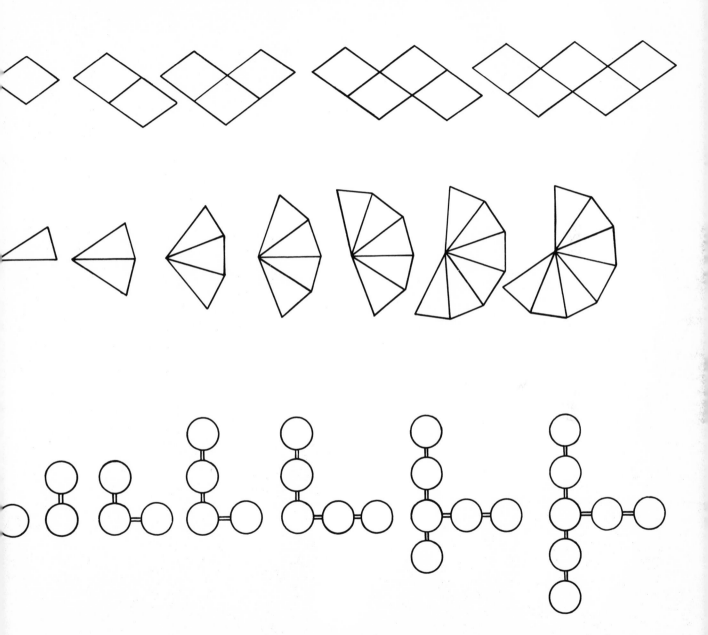

A book may have a shape as well as a pattern of opening. Sometimes this shape can tend toward a quality of sculpture which encourages the viewer to position it in different ways as well as to open it up sequentially. Yet however the book is positioned, it implies another position, and the viewer will tend to move it again.

31

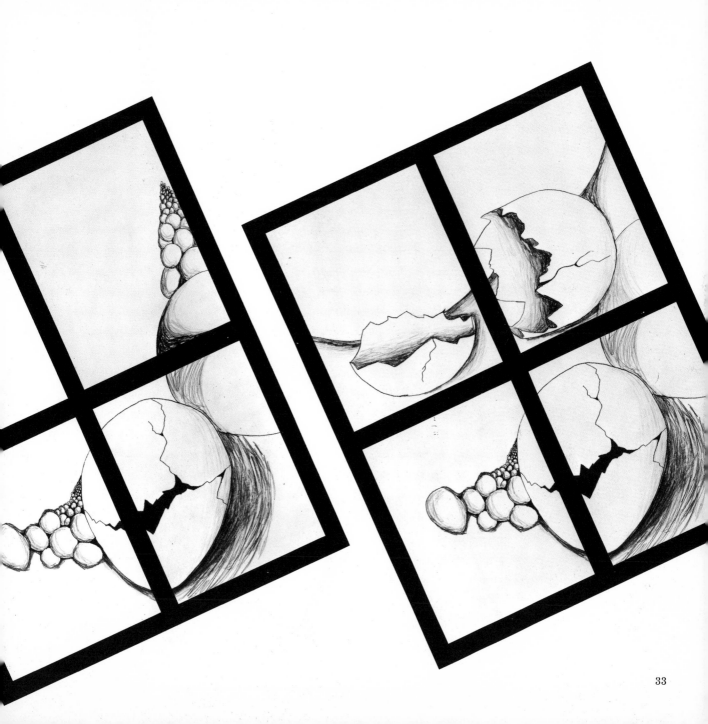

ny possible shapes for
ks have been shown
his chapter. However,
 intent is to encourage
 awareness of the
ential variety of new
pes.

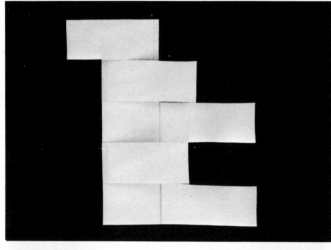

3.
Page Forms

fter a chapter on the variations of ok form, it is wise to devote some ne to the similar range of choice in lecting page form. In the same sense the book, the page is an opportunity discover new combinations of shapes, d whatever its arrangement, it is erely a device that is subservient to e form of the subject. Yet given at realization, it is still a vastly

undeveloped potential. In most book publication this is, of course, primarily due to cost factors. In the single-copy books we are designing, cost is irrelevant. So let the page, like the book itself, find a multitude of ways to meet the viewer. Most of the samples shown here are based on the rectangular page. Probably most efforts in making books

will be with the rectangular book, and it is this shape that is most in need of page variety. Remember that as the page changes, so the effect of the material on it changes. This can extend the range of a single image so that it can be seen more than one way, and it can also require a number of drawings of the same image to fit the many parts of the page.

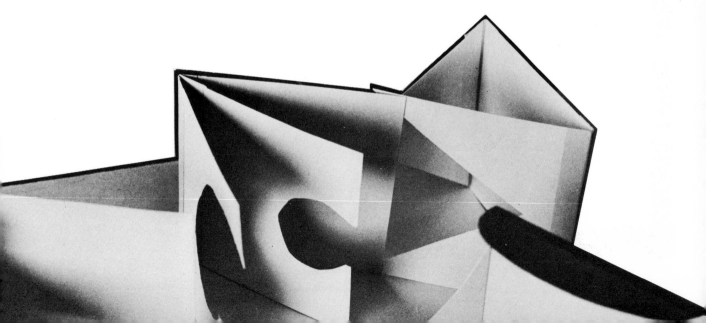

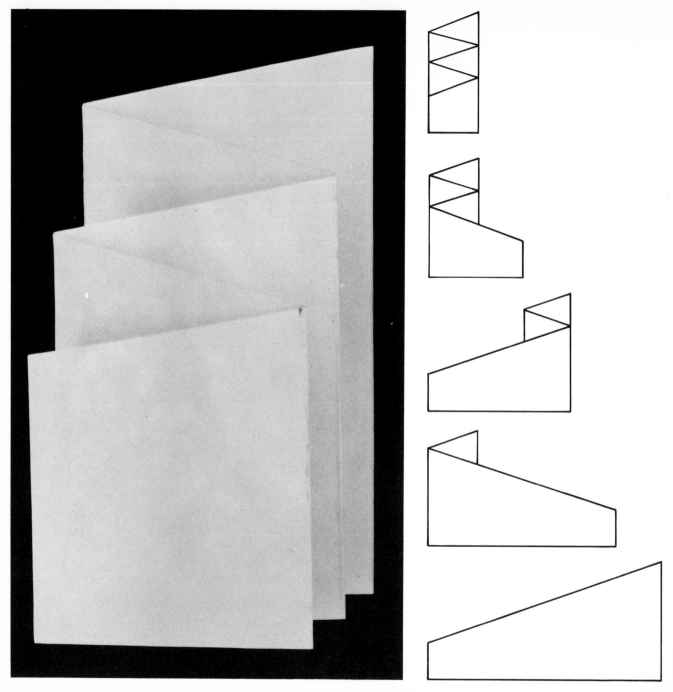

This book is folded rather than taped.

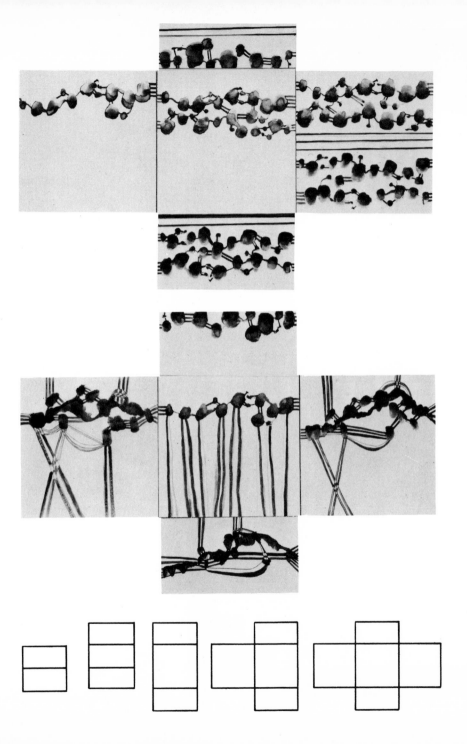

These samples are pages rather than whole books in the sense that they are easily incorporated into other, larger book forms. They do not deviate from the original image but rather encourage minor variation on the image as the page unfolds.

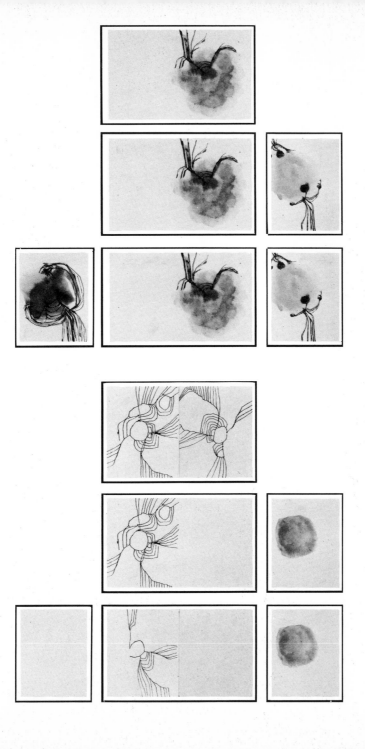

In the first page variation the page opens from itself to reveal an addition to the single image. In the second it opens to disclose a change from the original image. All of the alternatives on the facing page utilize the same basic image to indicate what happens to the image when the page shape changes.

4.
Page Design

How do you design a page? This question arises when the subject, book form, and page shape have been selected and the artist finally faces a blank space. The whole vastness of what has been done before in design is here to ponder upon, but that gives little solace to the designer making his first stroke on the page.

Initially, the whiteness and simplicity of the pure form must be changed, and the first group of illustrations in this chapter indicates some of the infinitude of choice. The page is changed—and yet it remains itself. All that we have done is play with the internal space. But the selection of how that space will be designed will effect whatever images are placed in the new space.

Besides flat space, there is also space with depth, space that expands or contracts, space that separates or unites images, space that comes to an abrupt halt, and space that leads on to the next page. Samples of these spatial phenomena are indicated in this chapter. But, just like space itself, none is overly definitive. Space by definition is alive and never more than relatively contained. Design of space is equally elusive, and its qualities should be felt as much as learned.

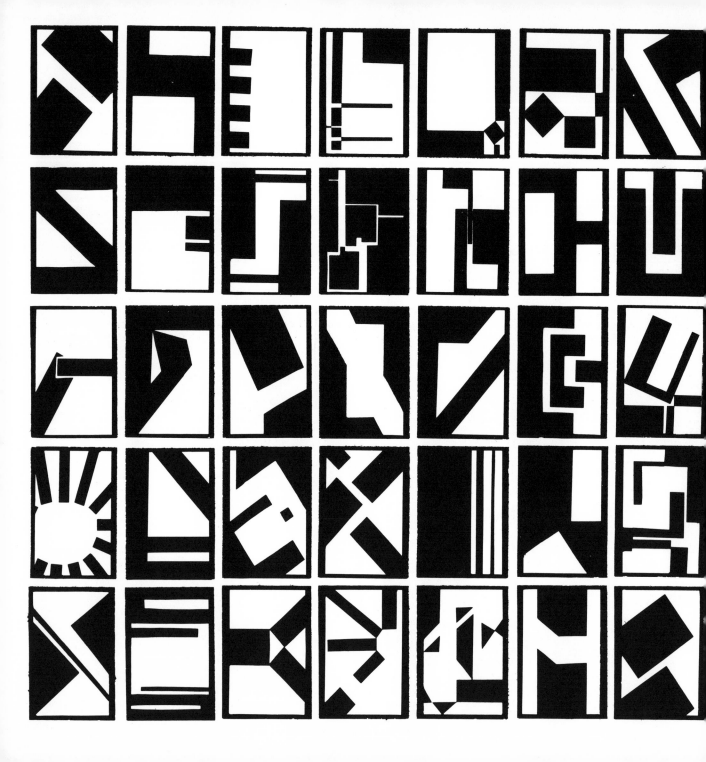

The design of a page is a bold experiment in visual dynamics. These fundamental divisions of space are all alive with the power to move the eye over the page as the designer wishes it to be moved. Before any other image is placed into the shapes, the shapes themselves must be sufficiently interesting and strong to merit holding an image.

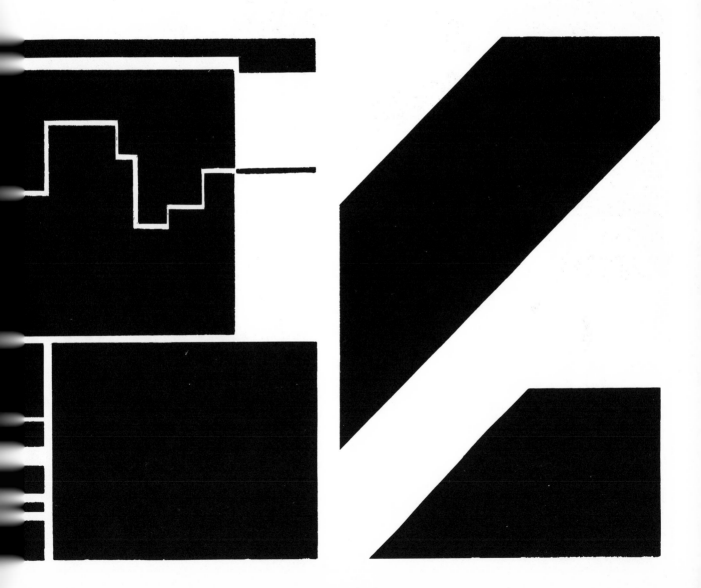

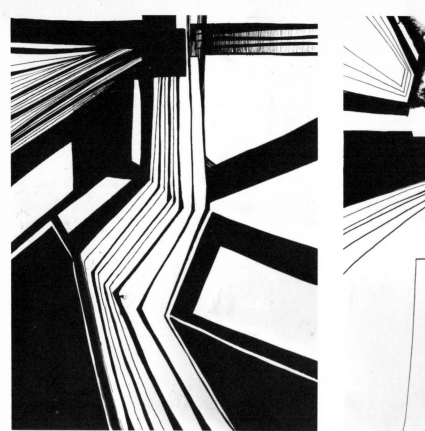

This is a series of studies for
the design of pages that vividly
incorporates image but is still clear
enough as page design to show
how the two elements are
complementary. These sketches in
ink, brush, and pen are free
and structured at the same time.
This makes for the best kind of
pulsating life in the tension
between form and motion.

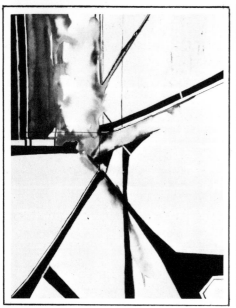

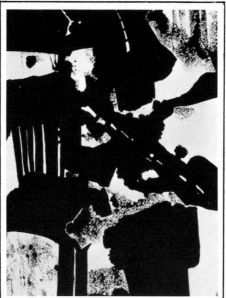
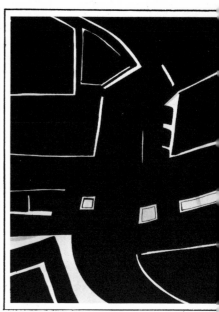

48

The particular interest of the two examples on this page is the fact that they are opposites. One is a study primarily in white left on a page of black and the other is black line on white. Both designs abound in motion and the desire of the line to spread out. In each case the design instinct is for the space to restrict the line. But the black line seems to move over the white space with more freedom than the white line over the black.

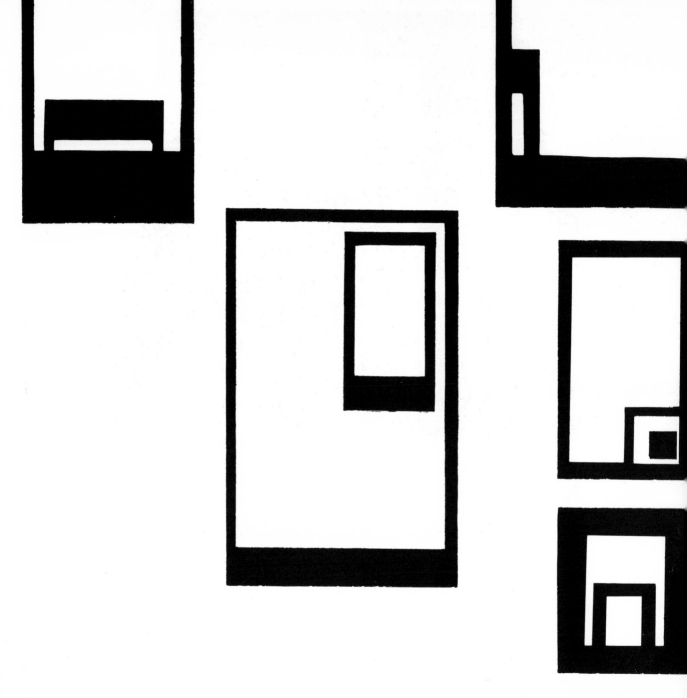

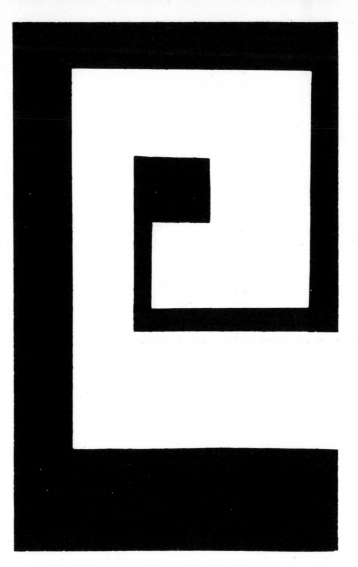

Another element of the design of a page is the depth relationship that can be created. These alternatives for the location of a rectangle show how it grows or changes character depending upon where it is placed, and the thickness of its sides and the sides of the larger rectangle. Any image placed in these different positions would be correspondingly different in effect.

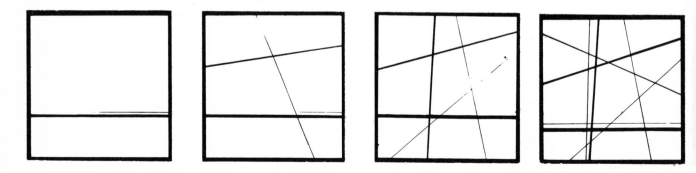

Line can be both the
design thrust or space
divider and the image
itself at the same time.
In fact it can do this
in a more natural
combination than, for
example, can image
using shading or shapes.
Line is a pure thing.
It is direction and shape
at the same time.

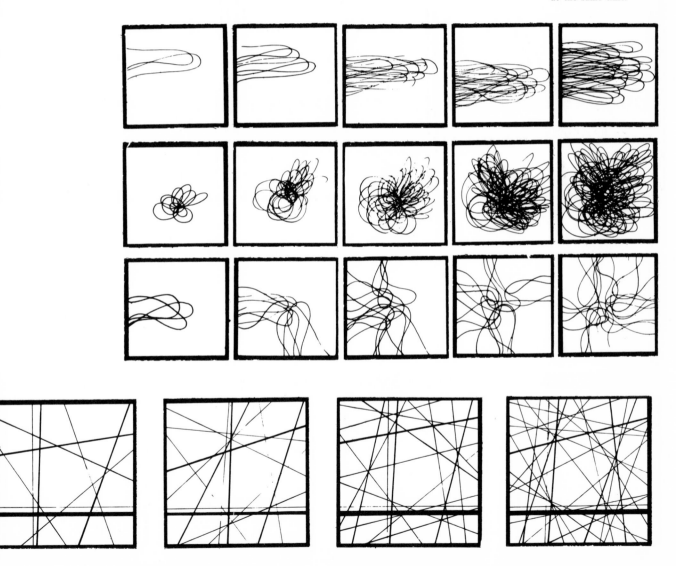

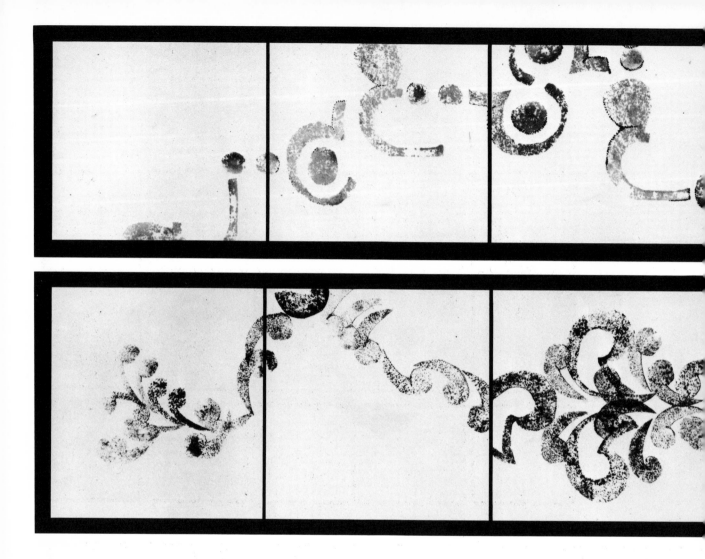

In sequential design each page is a design that has inference for the next page design. This does not mean that the pages should have the same amount of space utilization but that the shapes of the spaces should have a sort of generic relationship. To an extent this happens when the style is kept consistent. But it can also be emphasized, as in these series, when the form dances over the space linked from page to page.

5.
Growth

Growth is the essence of sequence. A picture-book is a device for teaching sequential vision, and the one paramount quality of this vision is that it is cumulative. Therefore the way the images grow from page to page is the very heart of this new vision.

How do things grow on a page? They can get larger or closer or darker or busier or branch off and multiply. They can start incomplete and fill in, or be barely visible and become clear. Each change in growth, whatever the particular method, produces expectation in the viewer. He follows the change to its logical or illogical end. As surprise variations and sudden spurts occur, he reacts to them. This gives the images life—life beyond the beauty or quality of their own form.

This is a fine example of a kind of growth, the growth of the innocuous into the gargantuan—the surprise growth of something into an unexpected dimension which changes its character. It is also an illustration of the growth of one object out of another.

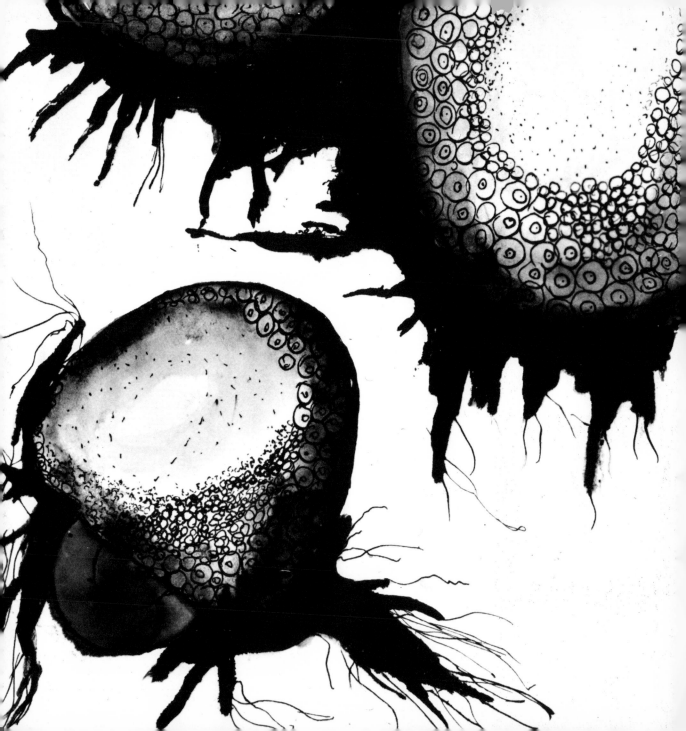

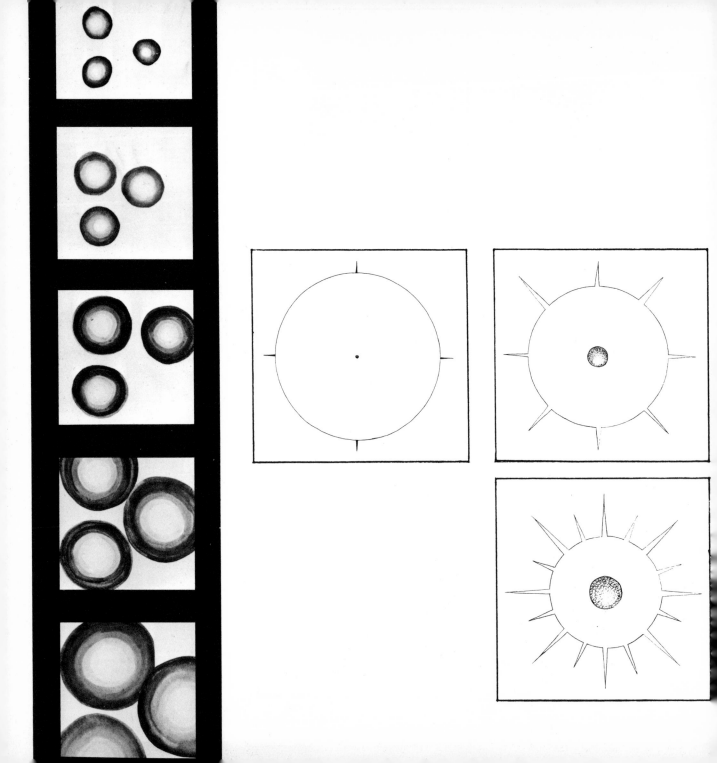

Any object, in this case the circle, is the potential base for a study in sequence and growth. The growth can simply move closer to the viewer, as in the sample on the far left, or it can both increase and decrease in complexity and size, like the other example. In the latter case four growth processes are taking place simultaneously.

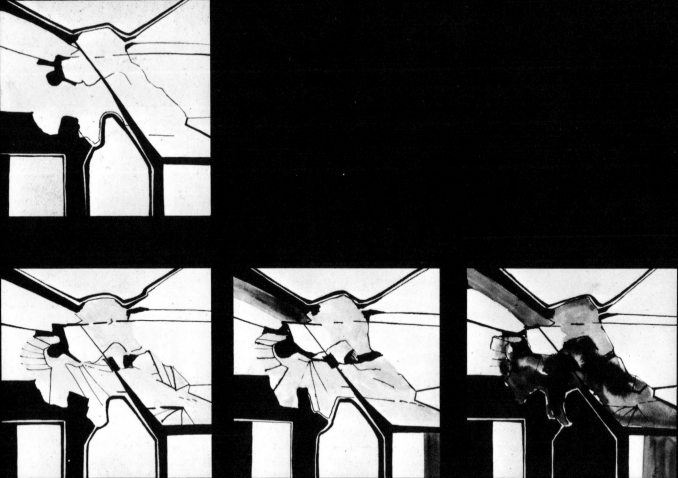

This growth process is from an open, light effect to a darker, closed result. The viewer can follow this growth to observe the change in mood and tension. It follows a natural inclination of change imposed upon itself by each previous change. But it is never precisely clear where that next change will occur, and some parts of the form advance too rapidly or even recede as if to challenge the basic direction of the growth.

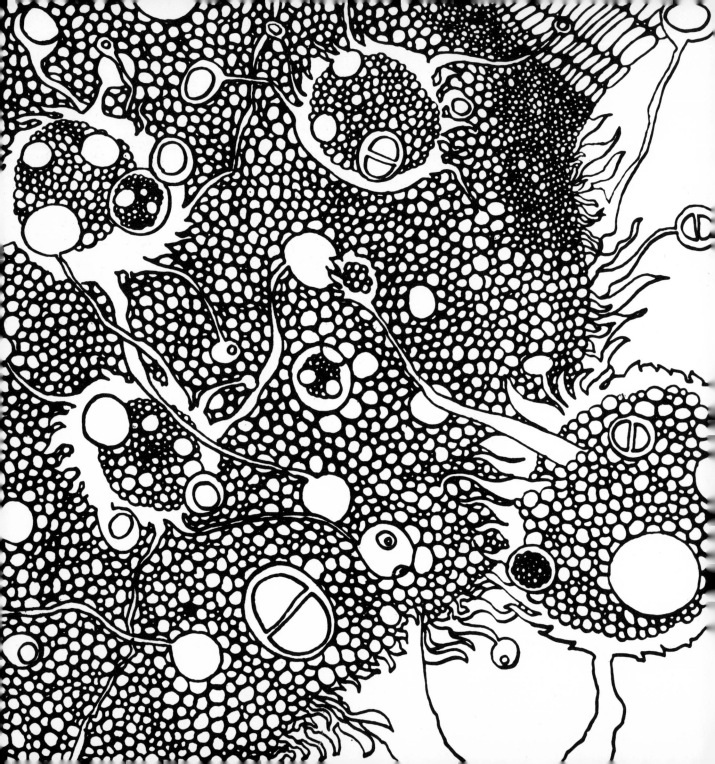

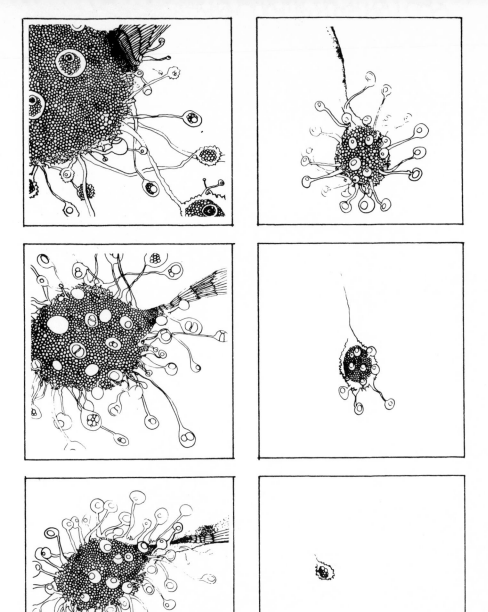

This is pure organic
growth in image form.
It is the growth of
form as it multiplies
itself cell by cell until it
becomes a new shape.
It crowds out space as
it grows and finally
threatens to engulf itself.
It is the moment when
a visual sequence
mirrors the sequence of
life.

6.
Materials

is chapter is concerned with the aterials used to make the picture-book. ch questions as should it be bound stitched or glued or taped appear levant. But do they make a difference, d is the difference significant? I member one teacher who had a whole ass meticulously measure and paste e cover and pages of a book; each one as then identical with the dimensions every other book in the class. If enticality is a virtue, then the project as a vast success.

I prefer to indicate ways to approach materials and then to let everyone show me how much cleverer they are than I would have been if I had been specific.

Materials are just tools, they are not products. Use the materials that are available. A cover could be done in metal or cardboard, felt or lace. String, rings, ribbon, tape, or glue as well as many other things can hold a book together. I happen to like tape.

It is simple to apply, or modify, or trim, or remove. It lasts reasonably well and can be applied so that the book opens in many directions. It is also contemporary in appearance. I am especially interested in the unfolding of a book, but one can also emphasize its textures or even decorate it with all sorts of appendages. However, a cover full of lace and pompoms still must open onto a series of pages. That is where it becomes a sequential rather than a sculptured object.

On these pages are three samples of effective materials to use in making books. The first is torn paper. It is obviously convenient to work with, since it can be rearranged until an interesting sequence is created. The second is images cut out of magazines. This is especially useful with theme books (discussed in the next chapter): it provides a multitude of images with which to organize a new relationship, a new logic of order. This logic is the creation of the designer rather than something dictated by the cut-out images themselves. The last suggestion is based on a woodcut—each repeated print is hand-painted to show a growth or change in the original image.

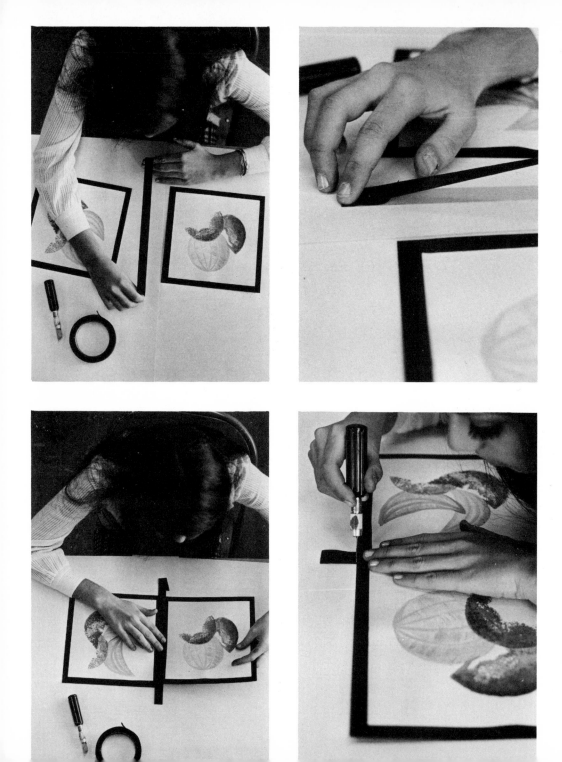

On this page is indicated the general process for facing a cover with some sort of decorative fabric. It involves cutting the fabric, gluing it to the front of the cover, turning it over and folding it flat at the corners, then gluing another piece of paper or one of the units from the sequence over the rough edges of the fabric. The facing page demonstrates the way to use tape to join pages of a book. The tape is placed on the table with the adhesive side facing up (but folded under on both ends to hold it in place) and then the pages are pressed onto it with a thin space left between them. Finally the extra tape is trimmed from both ends.

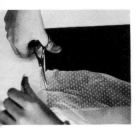

7.
Theme Books

he best way to show the value of ooks as a way of bringing the vision f people into contemporary perspective , of course, to show the books nemselves. This chapter will present nost of a book, thereby suggesting me of the quality of its impact.

The primary example chosen is a ook composed of construction paper and torn images from photo-journalism. It evokes the fragmentary nature of violence and the interplay of the many images of stress that move rapidly and fitfully across the eye of students in our media society.

These samples do not use all of the techniques this book has indicated are available to the designer. But that in itself points up the fact that each book has to incorporate only what it needs. A book is, I believe, more than just the sum of its images and devices. It holds them together for the purpose of making each talk to the other and in that dialogue creates a special impression on the mind of the viewer.

A young student made this book as a study of war. It is taken from assembled photos and put together to say something about his response. The dramatic quality of the study, besides its effect of catharsis, is the high level of design and order imposed upon such highly emotional material. It was designed as a theme book, and the challenge in such a case is to hold the material together despite its divergent sources.

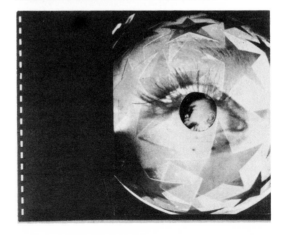

 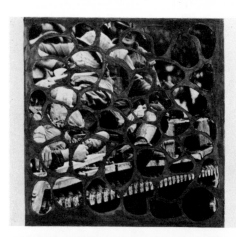

 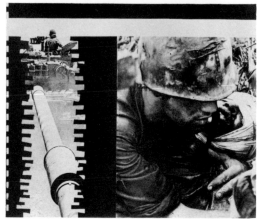

The mass-media magazines are an excellent source of material for theme books. The student is familiar with their content and usually eager to impose his own viewpoint upon their images. The primary device he uses to apply himself to these images is his personal design technique.

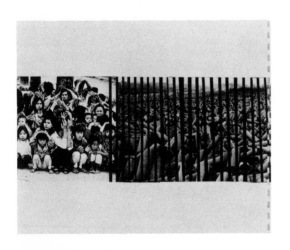

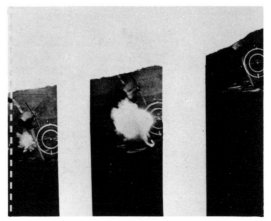

Notice how the use of intercutting
images together makes them
appear to blend into each other.
Or how images can become part
of a larger shape and can comment
on the larger shape in terms of
their own image. Especially
interesting to the concept of
linking image, theme, and design
is the placement of the total image
in the stage of an empty theater.
That example (on this page)
plays upon the double life of
image as both a projected image
and as reality.

The images on these and the next two pages are studies for a theme book on black-and-white design. The book is a flip book—each page flips up—but there are variations upon it that allow individual pages also to open up to the side or to both sides. As on the facing page, some see-through acetate pages are utilized. Sometimes the strength of the image comes from separating it by cutting it apart and then connecting it with line or new shapes. But the best results appear to come from the juxtaposition of the image with something unexpected.

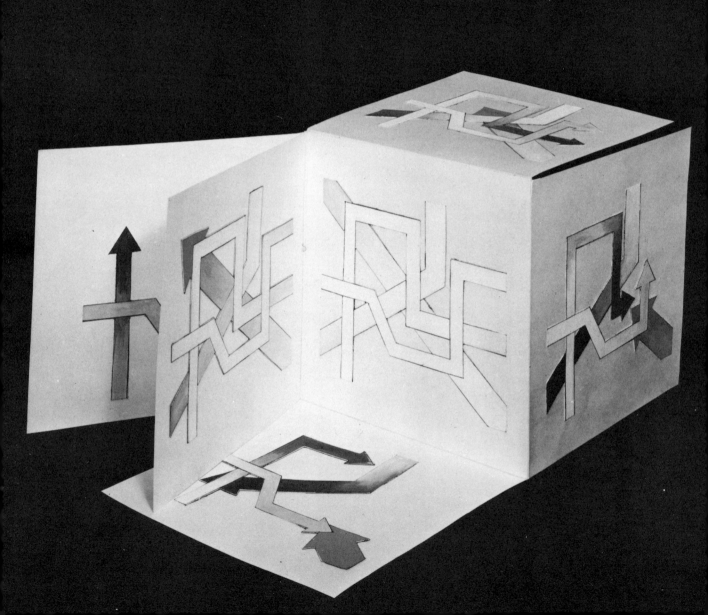

8.
A Gallery of Books

Most books are made to be read. Some are designed to be seen as well as read. The books on these pages were made to be more than seen: they are like modern sculpture, made to be touched and moved. They have a life created by the action of the viewer as he picks them up and turns them in many directions. They are, therefore, meant to be experienced: at best, photos can only suggest their nature.

On the facing page is a book that grows in the number of arrows that are on each page. The arrows imply the many ways the book can be opened.

These are a series of
sequence books opened
to their full extension.
When opened they can
either be seen a page
at a time or kept open
so that each new page
extends the length of
the book.

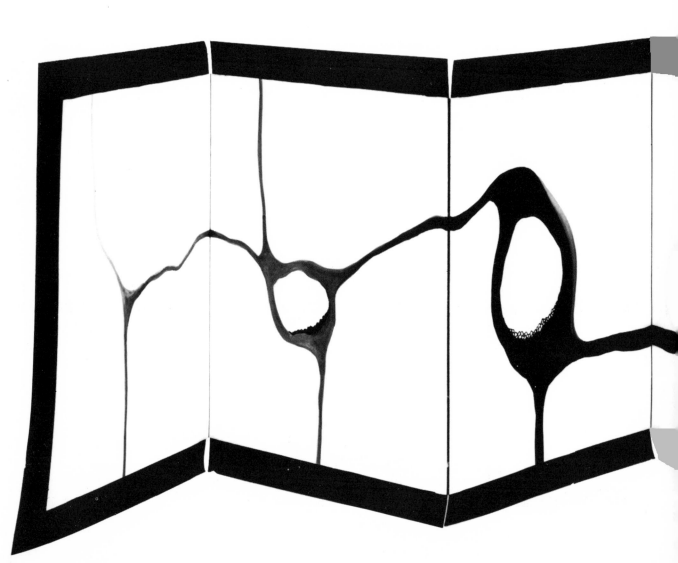

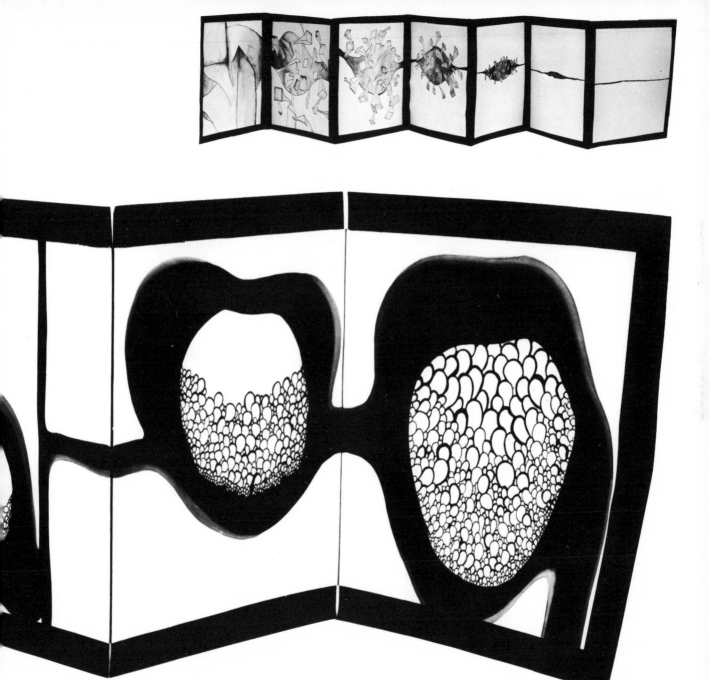

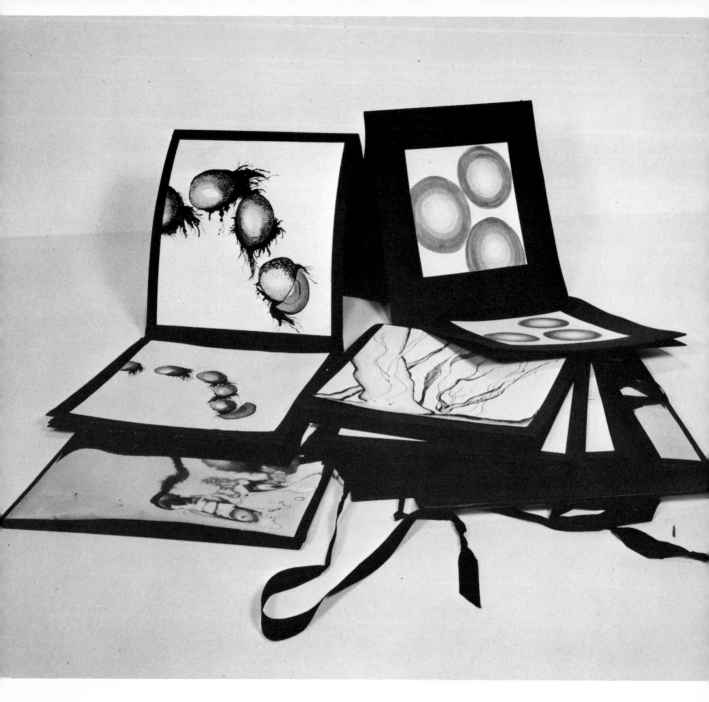

This is a sort of package book. It is a box that opens up to pour forth a number of sequence books.

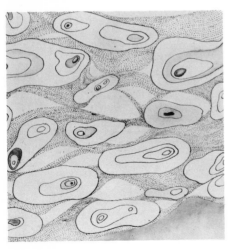
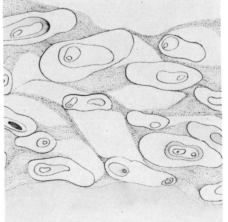
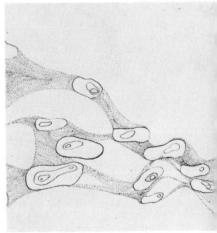

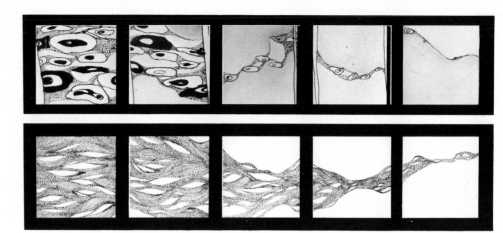

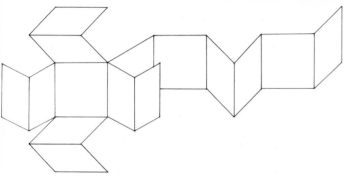

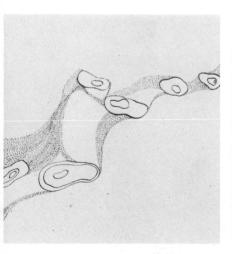

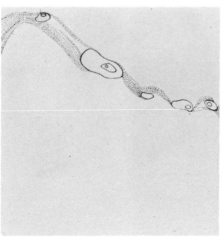

This is a kind of piggyback book that consists of a basic sequence book with two small sequence books attached to it. The smaller books are composed of the sketches for the basic book.

91

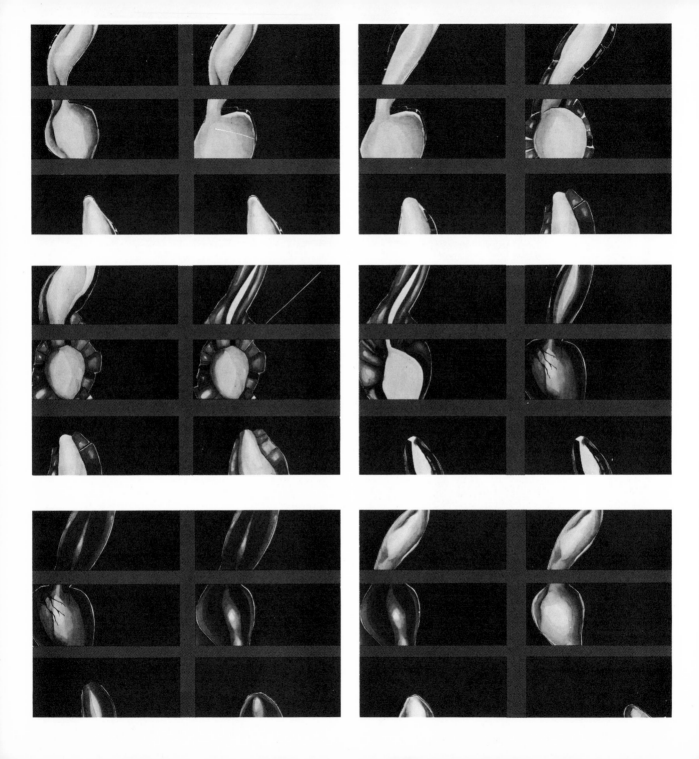

This book opens in each
direction on three levels.
As each part of each
page is turned it creates
a new variation on the
basic image. The
possibilities of that
variety are shown on
the facing page.

This picture-book opens
from one flat back page.
The whole sequence
is visible as each
individual variation is
turned. In contrast, the
book on the facing page
opens up from a
single circle, and as
it opens more circles
of design are seen.

This is a book in a case with the design sample on the cover of the case. The pages of the book, glued to pieces of cardboard to make them stiff, can be arranged in any way which pleases the viewer. The combinations the design can make are facilitated by the fact that the design reaches the edges of each square so that it matches the other squares at many points.